Schutz 5-D™

"Over the past few years, random-dot stereograms have been popping up all over the place. Unfortunately, most are very boring. Well, this has all changed with the release of the Blue Mountain Arts 5-D™ stereograms, developed by Dr. Stephen Schutz. In their flat format, they are works of art in their own right. When viewed in three dimensions, you will be amazed and delighted with the clarity and ingenious blending of theme. No more patterns of endless dots. Every Blue Mountain Arts print is a blend of familiar objects or pleasing geometric patterns, and the 3-D image you will soon see is sure to delight. But be forewarned, this will be habit-forming, and you will be begging Blue Mountain Arts® to come out with more, more, and more."

—Sheldon Aronowitz
Writer, *Stereo World* magazine
and Owner of the largest
3-D collection in the world

"Susan Polis Schutz has reached a kind of gemlike and crystalline form... One picks up Susan's poetry and reads it to the quiet and tasteful accompaniment of Stephen's art and suddenly you are with friends you want to know and speak with more."

—*The Saturday Evening Post*

"Susan Polis Schutz remains one of the most popular poets in America today, and her work touches virtually everyone."

—Associated Press

"Blue Mountain Arts of Boulder, Colorado, exploded out of the gates with... 5-D™ stereograms. Blue Mountain Arts... is the creation of the husband and wife team, Stephen Schutz, who combined an interest in art with a doctorate in theoretical physics, and Susan Polis Schutz, a widely published author of love poetry."

—Steve Woodward, *The Oregonian*

"Susan and Stephen have sold 200 million cards and 10 million poetry and inspirational books."

—*The New York Times*

How to see the hidden 5-D™ stereogram image:
Read instructions on next page.

What is a 5-D™ stereogram?

A stereogram is a computer-generated image that "pops out" of the paper as if it were a Multi-Dimensional object. In order to see this image, however, the stereogram must be viewed in a certain way.

In the 1950s, people wore red and green glasses to see movies and pictures in 3-D. In 1960, Bela Julesz at Bell Laboratories invented the random-dot stereogram, which enabled people to see 3-D images without special glasses by taking advantage of the way our brain interprets depth.

Dr. Stephen Schutz, artist and physicist, recently pioneered a new technique and authored a program that produces Multi-Dimensional images from real artwork rather than from random dots. By removing the random dots from stereograms, Dr. Schutz has raised the art of the stereogram to a new level of aesthetic beauty — the 5-D™ stereogram.

Each page of artwork in this book has a hidden Multi-Dimensional image waiting to be discovered by you. Just follow the directions below, and you will experience a truly astounding form of interactive art.

How to see the hidden 5-D™ stereogram image:

Hold the art close to your nose so that it appears blurry. Relax and stare at it. Make believe you are looking "through" the art. Slowly move it away from your face until an image "pops out" and becomes perfectly clear. The time it takes to see the image can vary, so don't get discouraged!

Alternate viewing method: Place a sheet of plastic or glass over the page so that you can see your own reflection. Hold the art at arm's length and focus on your reflection in the plastic or glass until the 5-D™ stereogram image begins to "pop out."

Important: If you experience any discomfort, then stop, rest, and try again later.

Love in 5-D™ Stereograms

**Contains Phenomenal
Hidden Multi-Dimensional Images**

**Created by Stephen Schutz, Ph.D.,
with Poetry by Susan Polis Schutz**

Each page of artwork in this book has a hidden 5-D™ stereogram picture
waiting to be discovered by you.
But first, please read the directions on the facing page.

Blue Mountain Press®
Boulder, Colorado

Mail Order

Most of the 5-D™ stereograms published in this book are available on greeting cards, prints, and calendars.

Due to the enormous popularity of Blue Mountain Arts' products, you may find that your local stores are temporarily out of the designs you desire. If this should happen, we welcome your mail-order inquiries.

Write to us for information:

Blue Mountain Arts, Inc.
Mail Order
P.O. Box 4549
Boulder, CO 80306
(303) 449-0536

The following people are to be thanked for their valuable contribution to this book: Faith Gowan, Jody Kauflin, Norine Neely, Jan Betts, Doug Pagels, John Crane, Patty Brown, Ed Guzik, Mark Rinella, Matt Rantanen, and Jared Schutz.

ISBN: 0-88396-389-2
Library of Congress Catalog Card Number: 94-20661

Library of Congress Cataloging-in-Publication Data

Schutz, Susan Polis.
  Love in 5-D™ stereograms/ created by Stephen Schutz: with poetry by Susan Polis Schutz.
      p.   cm.
  ISBN 0-88396-389-2 : $17.95
  1. Schutz. Stephen. 2. Computer art — United States. 3. Optical illusions in art. 4. Love in art. 5. American poetry—20th century. I. Schutz, Stephen. 5-D stereogram. II. Title. III. Title: Love in five-D.
N7433.85.S38A37 1994
760—dc20   94-20661
                                                CIP

Printed in Hong Kong
First Printing: June, 1994

Blue Mountain Press ®

P.O. Box 4549, Boulder, Colorado 80306

Introduction

Love is the most important feeling in the world. It is the source of strength, unity, harmony, passion, and truth.

Love in 5-D_{TM} Stereograms is Stephen's and my expression of what love is in poetry and Multi-Dimensional illustrations. The mystical phenomenon of Stephen's sensitive graphics, with meaningful hidden images, brings the art of the stereogram to a new level of aesthetic beauty.

This year, Stephen and I celebrated 25 years of a fantastic marriage, and we continue to love each other more every day. *Love in 5-D_{TM} Stereograms* is a celebration of love.

"Love is the source of life"

Susan Polis Schutz

Love is...

...being happy for the other person when they are happy
being sad for the person when they are sad
being together in good times
and being together in bad times

Love is the source of strength

5-D™ Stereogram Image: "Love in Flight"

…being honest with yourself at all times
being honest with the other person at all times
telling, listening, respecting the truth
and never pretending

Love is the source of reality

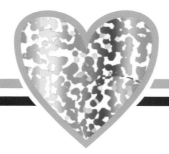

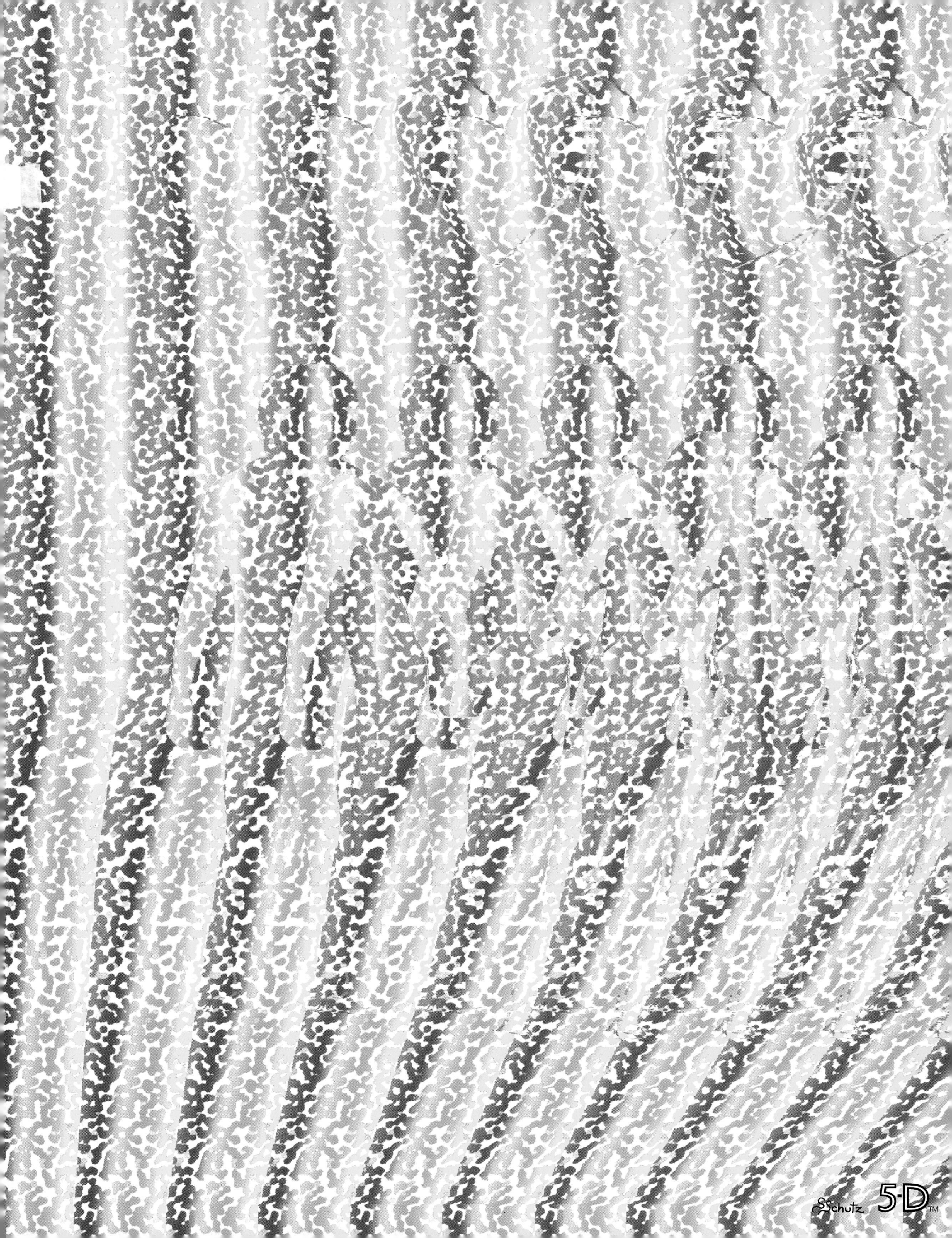
Schutz
5-D™

Love is...

...an emotion
   that makes your
   body more alive
   your soul more tender
   and your life more beautiful

Love is the source of sensitivity

Love is...

...the freedom to pursue your own desires
   while sharing your experiences with the other person
   the growth of one individual alongside of
   and together with the growth of another individual

Love is the source of success

5-D™ Stereogram Image: "Birds in Friendship"

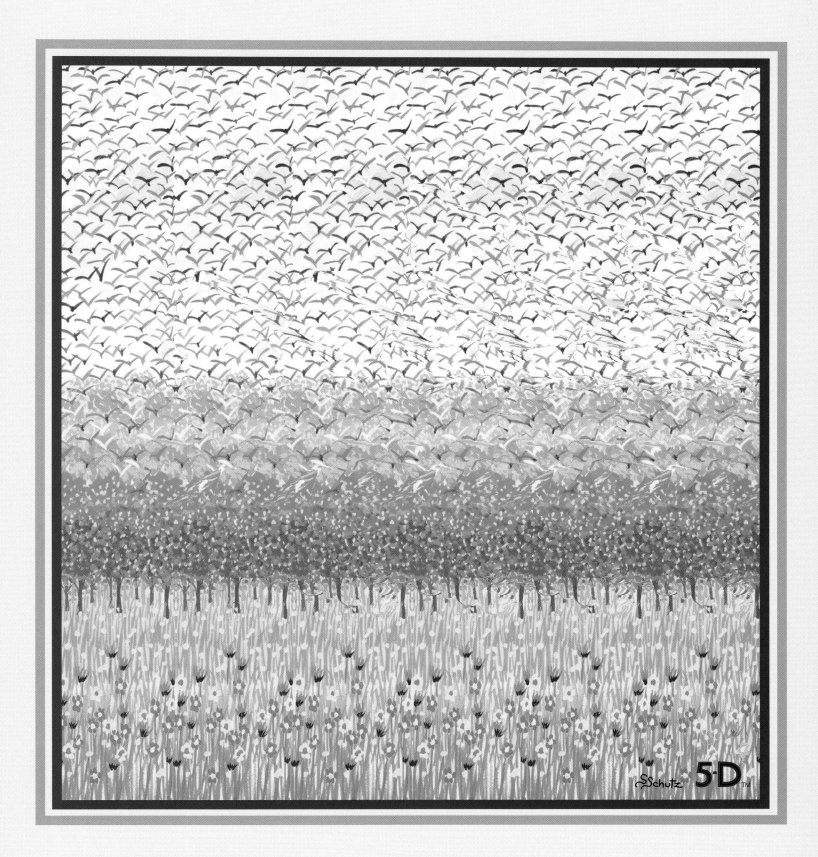

Love is...

...an understanding so complete that
 you feel as if you are a part of the other person
 accepting the other person just the way they are
 and not trying to change them to be something else

Love is the source of unity

5-D™ Stereogram Image: "Playful Dolphins"

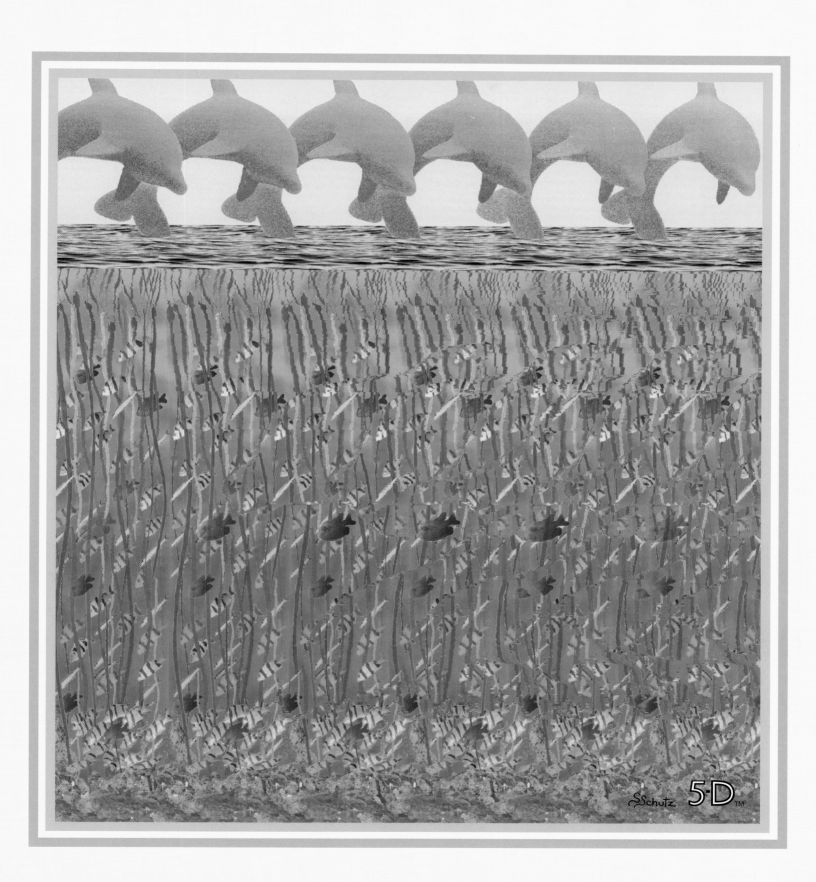

Love is ...

...not an excuse to stop growing

    not an excuse to stop making yourself better

    not an excuse to lessen one's goals

    not an excuse to take the other person for granted

Love is the source of commitment

5-D ™ Stereogram Image: "I Love You"

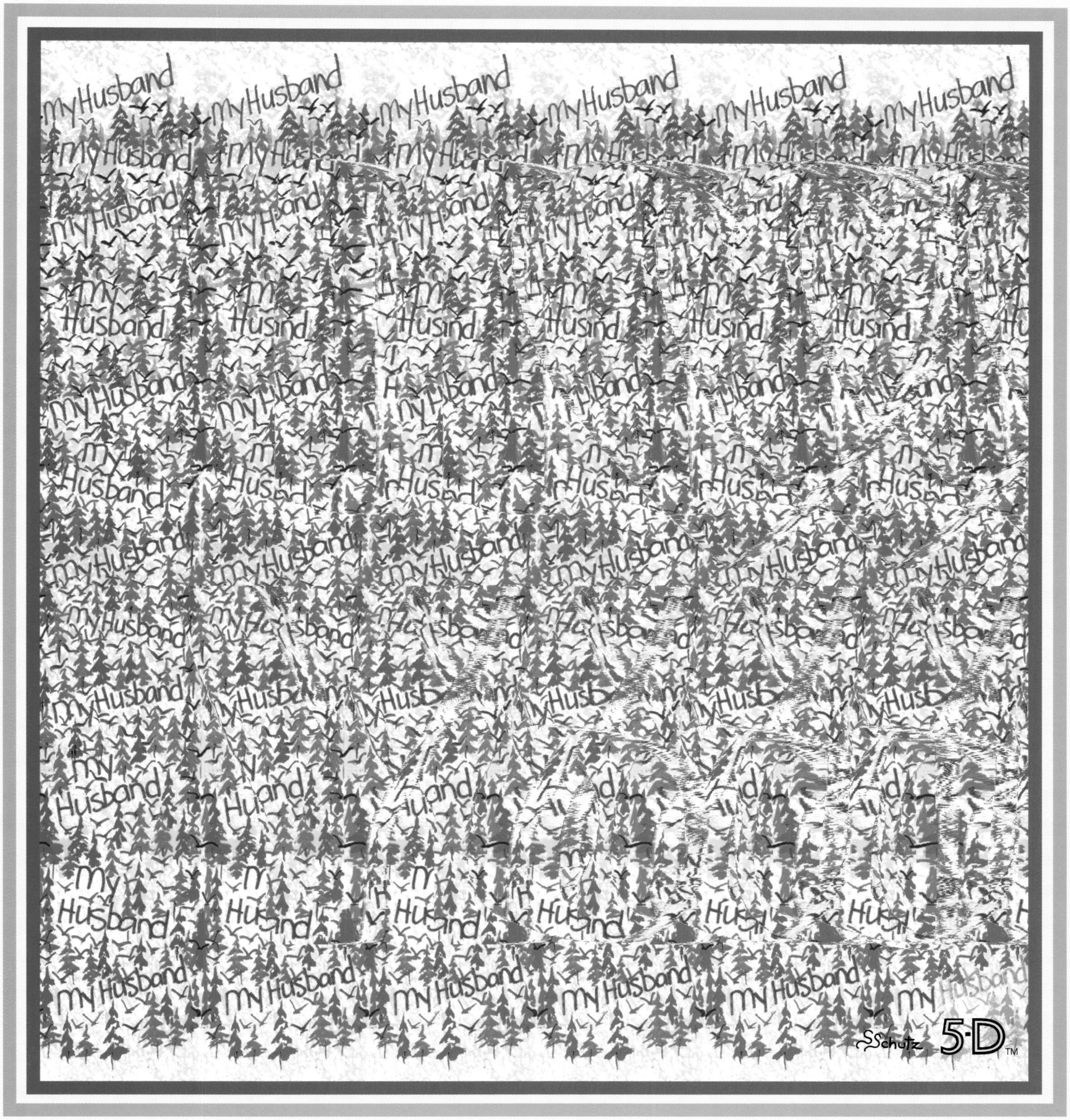
My Husband
SSchutz
5-D™

Love is ...

...following dreams together
working towards common goals
sharing responsibilities

Love is the source of harmony

5-D ™ Stereogram Image: "Paper Dolls Encircling Earth"

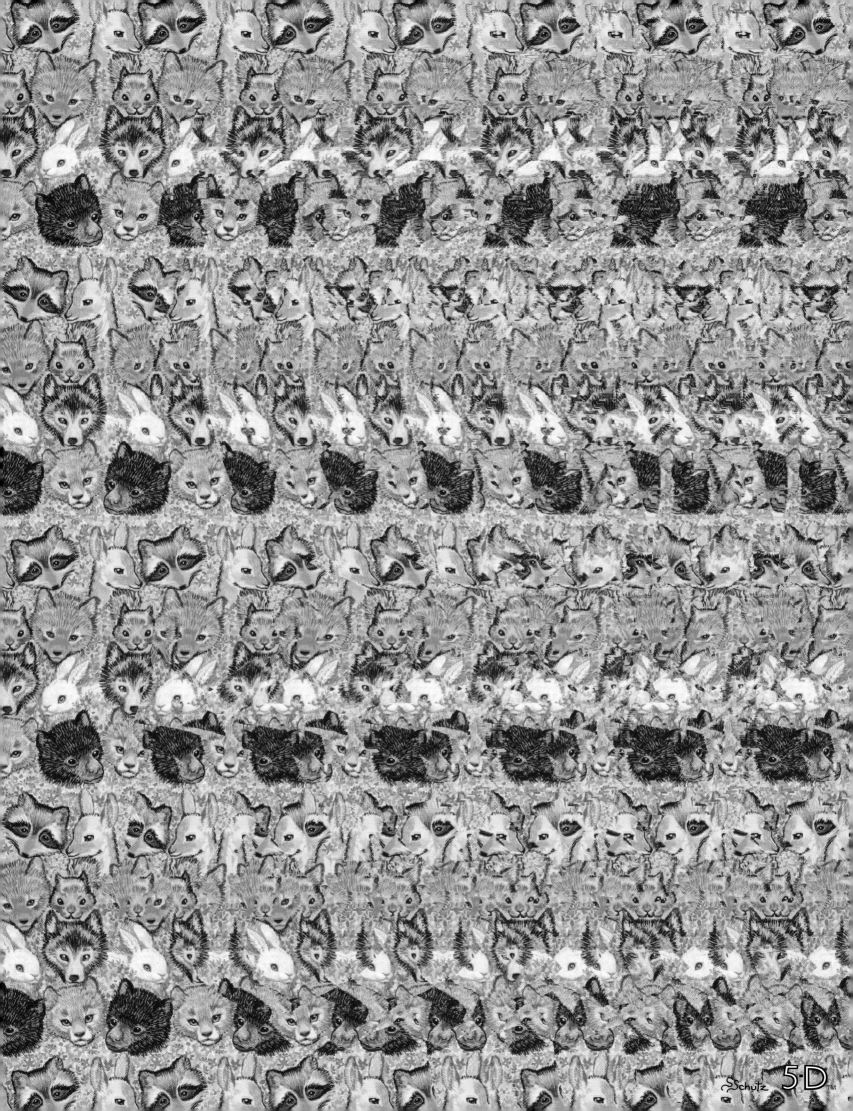

Love is . . .

...not a feeling
to be taken lightly
Love is
a feeling
to be cherished
nurtured and cared for

Love is the source of sacredness

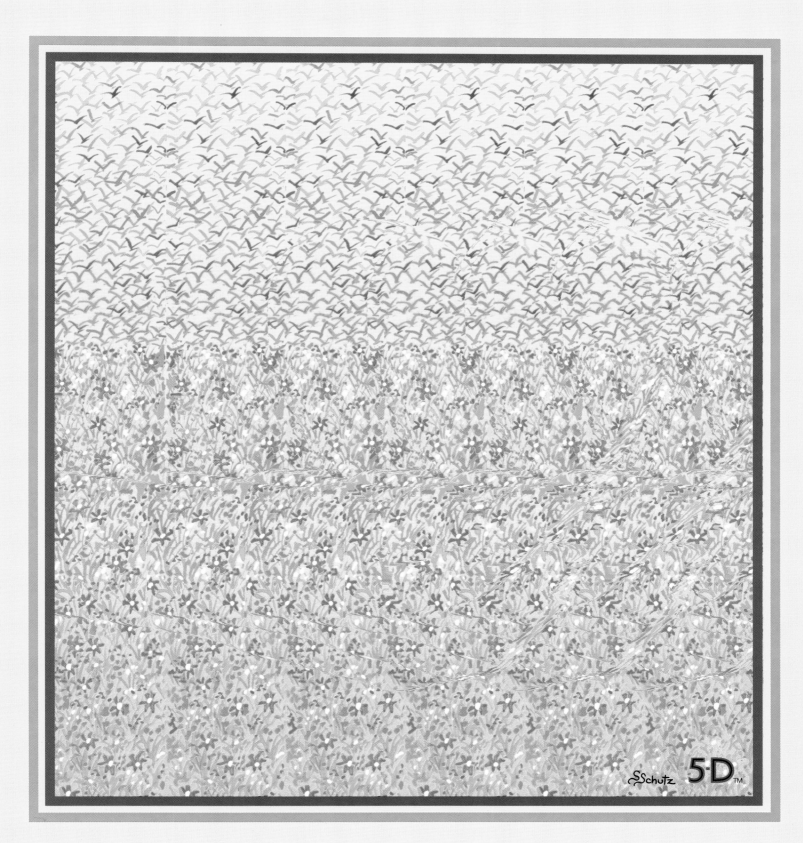

5-D™ Stereogram Image: "Hearts"

Love is . . .

...finding peaceful solutions to problems
finding common interests
finding ways to help others

Love is the source of hope

5-D ™ Stereogram Image: "A Flower of Hope"

Love is...

...the melody of the heart
the voice of the spirit

Love is the source of inspiration

5-D™ Stereogram Image: "Mountain of Love"

Love is ...

...an all-encompassing affection
an extreme force
an overwhelming excitement

Love is the source of intensity

5-D ™ Stereogram Image: "Dancer Holding a Ribbon"

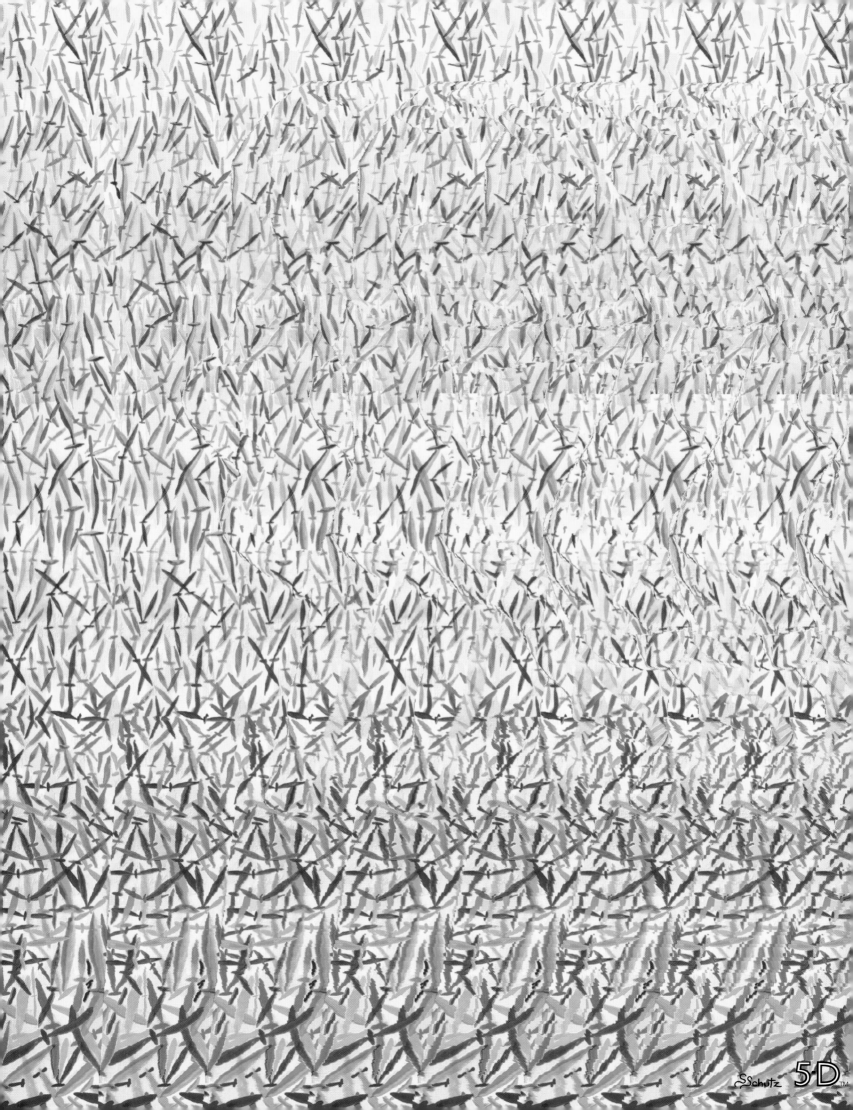

Love is...

...a walk in fantasy
a dance in nature

Love is the source of dreams

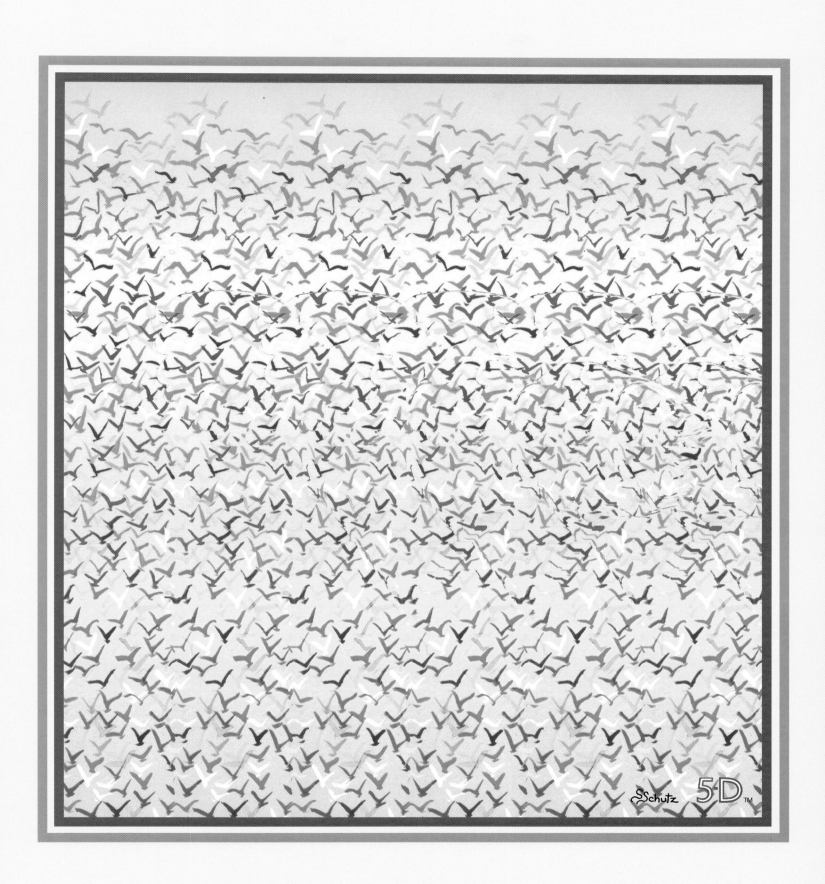

Love is . . .

...thinking together
planning together
carrying out ideas together

Love is the source of the future

5-D ™ Stereogram Image: "You're a Star"

Love is ...

...giving and taking in a daily situation
being patient with each other's needs and desires

Love is the source of sharing

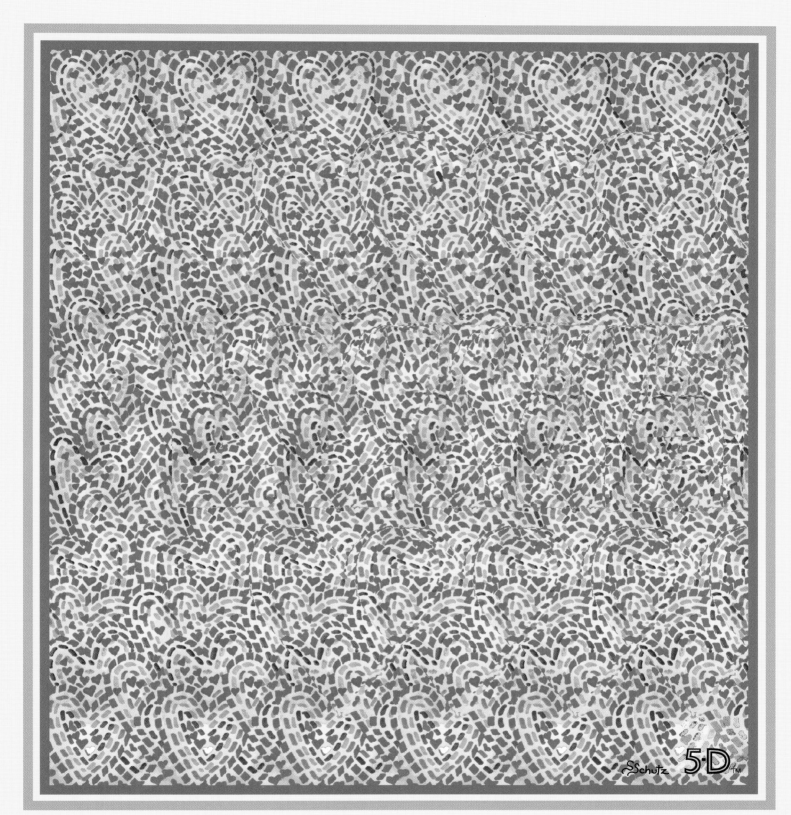

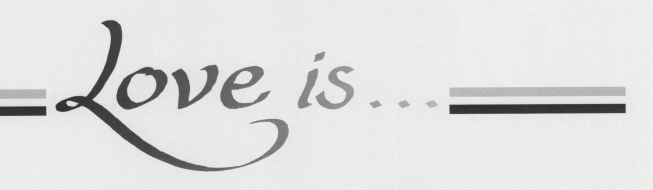

Love is ...

...the deepest concern
the union of two individuals

Love is the source of friendship

5-D™ Stereogram Image: "Hands of Friendship"

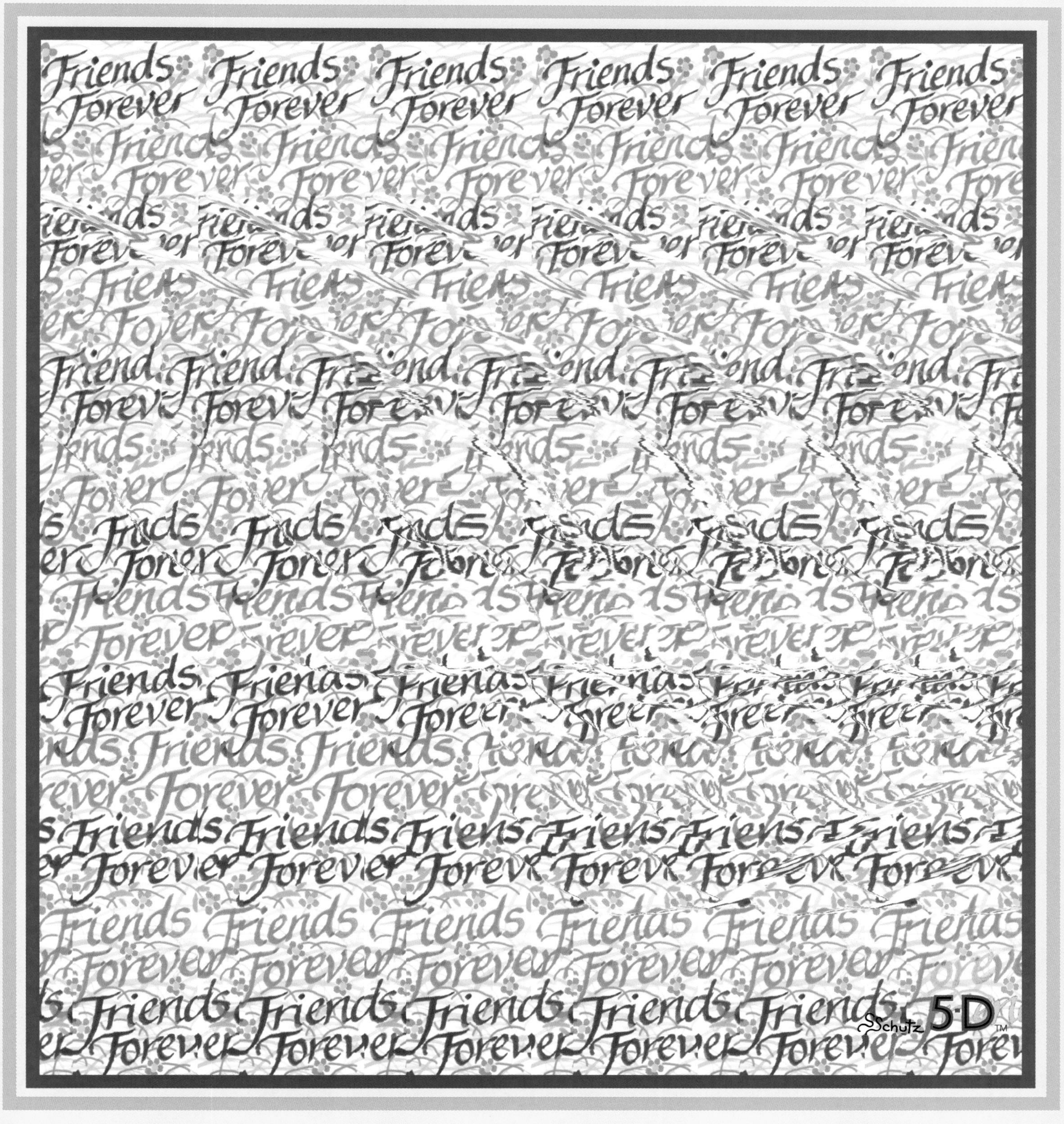
Friends
Forever
Schutz
5-D ™

Love is ...

...an explosion of
every fiber
every nerve

Love is the source of celebration

5-D™ Stereogram Image: "Special Star"

Love is...

...the fury of the storm
the calm in the rainbow

Love is the source of passion

5-D™ Stereogram Image: "Rainbow"

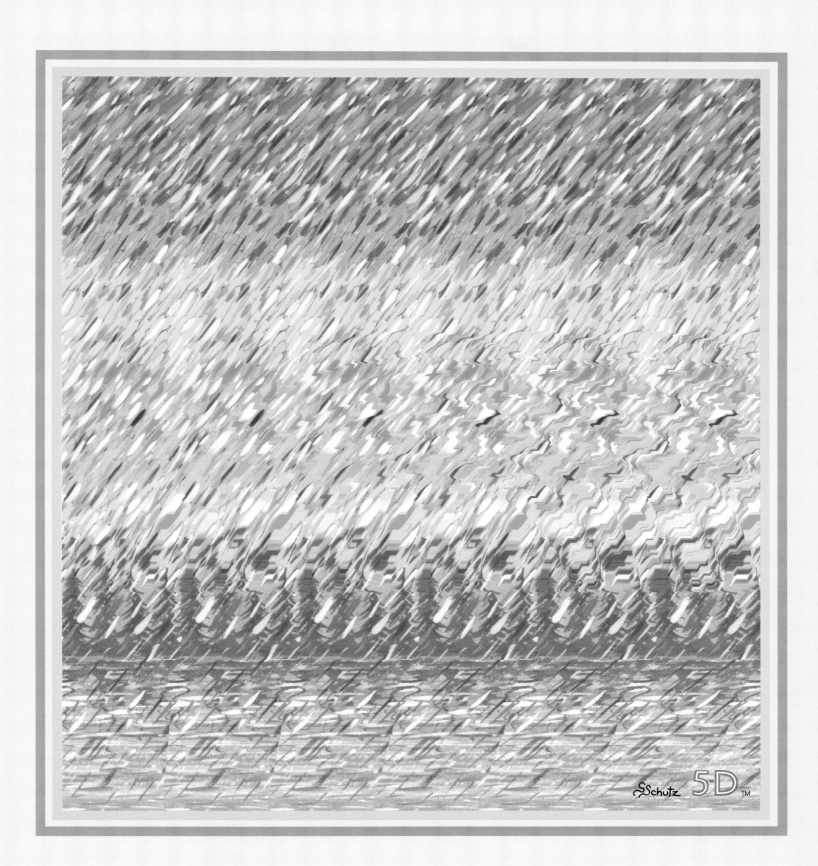

Love is . . .

...knowing that the other person
will always be with you regardless of what happens
missing the other person when they are away
but remaining near in heart at all times

Love is the source of security

5-D ™ Stereogram Image: "You Are in My Heart"

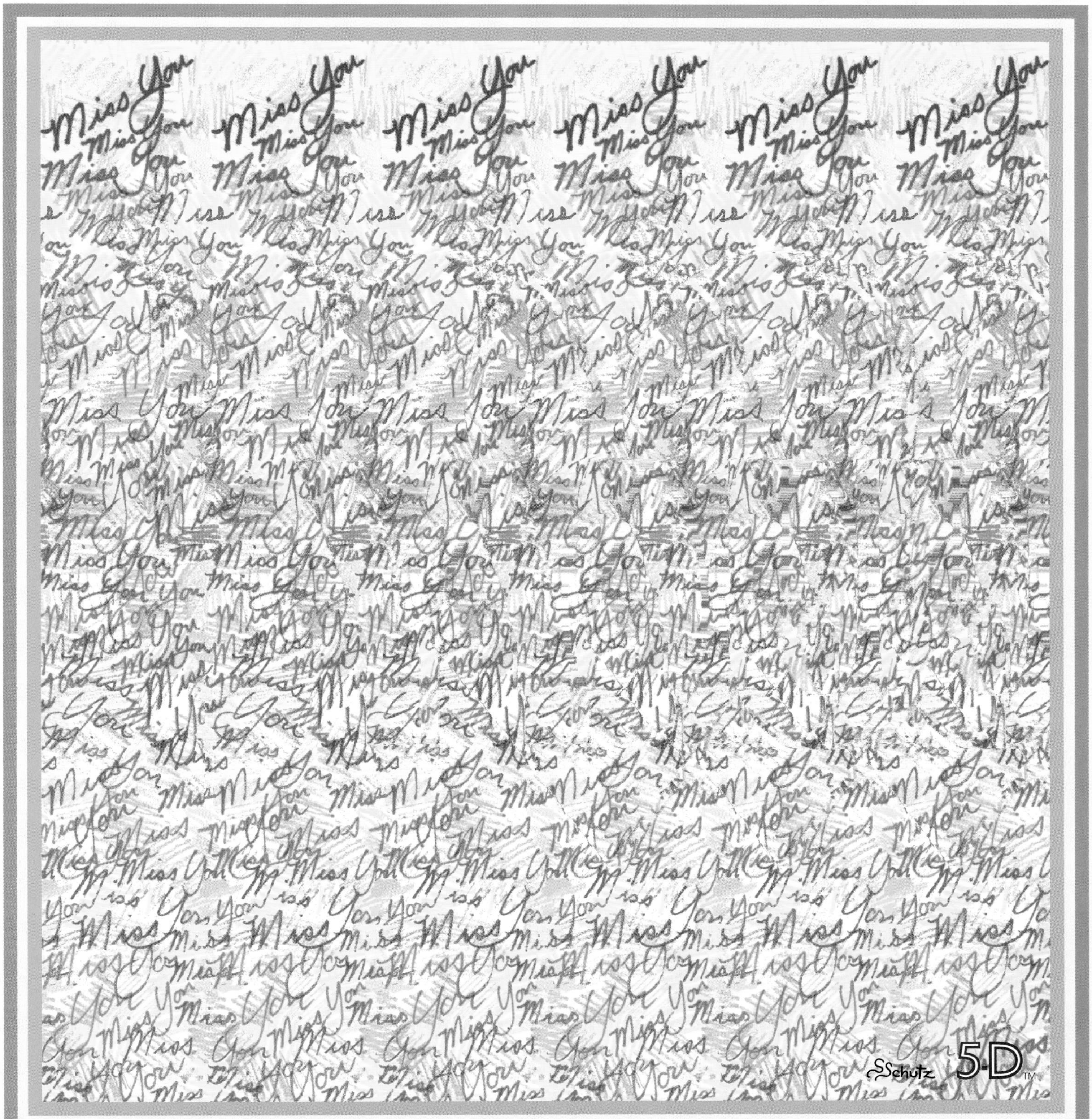
Miss You
Schutz
5-D™

Love is . . .

...the source of life

5-D™ Stereogram Image: "Love"

Seeing in Stereo

Dr. Stephen Schutz Takes the Art of the Stereogram to a New Aesthetic Level

Recent improvements in computer technology have enabled the famous artist (and physicist) Dr. Stephen Schutz to pass a new threshold of innovation and liberate art from its prior two-dimensional limitations. "Spectacular!" says Leonard Nimoy about 5-D™ stereograms. "Beautiful and often dazzling works of art," says Dick Kreck of *The Denver Post.* And from Sheldon Aronowitz, the owner of the largest 3-D collection in the world: "Finally, a refreshing improvement in dimensional images—pictures you will find yourself getting 'lost' in—pictures that will put the word 'WOW!' back in your vocabulary."

5-D™ stereograms, Stephen Schutz's most recent artistic creation, effectively establish a genre of Multi-Dimensional art. Stereograms had their origins in 1960 when Bela Julesz developed the "random-dot stereogram" as a tool to study perceptual psychology. For the past thirty years, primitive random-dot stereograms have relied on repetitive textures to disguise hidden three-dimensional images.

Stephen Schutz's 5-D™ stereograms have successfully replaced random-dot textures with incredible artwork, which makes 5-D™ stereograms "dimensional dynamite," in the words of David Hutchinson of the National Stereoscopic Association. Dr. Schutz's full-color base-art foregrounds (what everyone sees on the surface) are attractions in and of themselves. When this foreground is dramatically supplemented by a hidden image that relates and interacts with it, the exquisite result comes alive as wolves leap off the page and stars hang in a multi-layered sky. Stephen Schutz's accomplishment is a testimony to what can happen when the creative envelope of art is expanded and enhanced by the cutting edge of technology.

"Over the past few years, random-dot stereograms have been popping up all over the place. Unfortunately, most are very boring," notes 3-D collector and writer for *Stereo World* magazine, Sheldon Aronowitz. "This has all changed with the release of the Blue Mountain Arts 5-D™ stereograms developed by Dr. Stephen Schutz. In their flat format, they are works of art in their own right. When viewed in three dimensions, you will be amazed and delighted with the clarity and ingenious blending of theme. No more patterns of endless dots."

This intriguing image represents how the computer "sees" Stephen Schutz's Multi-Dimensional image that appears at the front and back of this book. The computer uses colors to designate dimensional levels; objects on the same level are of the same color. The computer then integrates these color levels with the chosen background art and transforms them into 5-D™ stereograms by applying Stephen Schutz's advanced programmed formula.

About the Artist and Author

Stephen Schutz is an artist and a physicist, a rare combination of talents emanating from the mind and heart. Enraptured at an early age with beauty and aesthetic form, Stephen pursued the paths of science and art simultaneously. He graduated from the famous High School of Music and Art in New York City, and studied physics at M.I.T. and Princeton University, where he received a Ph.D. in theoretical physics in 1970. While pursuing advanced scientific learning, Stephen continued to develop his artistic abilities at the Museum of Fine Arts in Boston.

During college, Stephen met and fell in love with the woman who was to become his equal loving partner in marriage, family, and art. In1969, Susan Polis Schutz and Stephen Schutz moved to the mountains of Colorado where Susan was a freelance writer and Stephen researched solar energy at a government research laboratory. On the weekends, they began experimenting with printing Susan's poems surrounded by Stephen's art on posters that they silk-screened in their basement. From the very start, their love of life and for one another touched a receptive chord in people everywhere. The public's discovery of the creative collaboration of Susan Polis Schutz and Stephen Schutz set the stage for a world-wide love affair with their works.

"Susan Polis Schutz remains one of the most popular poets in America today," reports the Associated Press, "and her work touches virtually everyone." Her honest and compelling poems have a universal appeal. As a frequent visitor to the bestseller lists, Susan and Stephen's books and poetry cards have touched the hearts of over 200 million people, and Susan's verse has been translated into many foreign languages. Susan is living proof that love and friendship are the universal languages, and she continues to find new ways to share her thoughts through her peaceful and inspiring poems.

As Susan's achievements have grown, so too have Stephen's. His instinctive curiosity about the way things work keeps him evolving as an artist, as a scholar, and as a person. An important part of the evolutionary process for all of us has been the computer. Stephen began working with a computer in the early 1960s when, according to Stephen, "You didn't even see the actual computer because it was tucked away somewhere in the building, taking up an entire room. Now a desktop computer can perform functions in a minute that required countless hours for the huge early machines to perform."

Because Stephen is an artist, computer whiz, and innovator, there is no one better suited to take the art of the stereogram to its next level. Combine that with the fact that it would be difficult to discover a poet with a more significant following than Susan Polis Schutz, who *TIME* magazine referred to as the "reigning star... in high-emotion." Together, Susan and Stephen Schutz's most recent books, featuring Susan's poetic messages and Stephen's 5-D™ stereograms, are just the latest in a series of beautiful contributions the couple has made over the past 25 years.

Photo by Jared